May your birthday
be meowgical!

Blank Classic

Name ____

Address ____

____

____

____

____

The Happy Birthday Dotted Bullet Journal
113 numbered pages - 120 total pages
A5 (5.83 x 8.27)

Design © 2020 Blank Classics

All rights reserved. No part of this book
may be stored in a retrieval system,
reproduced or transmitted in any form
or by any other means without written
permission from the publisher or a
licence from the Canadian Copyright
Licensing Agency.

Blank Classic

Mailing address:
Blank Classic
PO BOX 4608
Main Station Terminal
349 West Georgia Street
Vancouver, BC
Canada, V6B 4A1

Cover design by: A.R. Roumanis

ISBN: 978-1-77437-905-9

FIRST EDITION / FIRST PRINTING

— Contents —

Page	Topic
Page	

— Contents —

Page	Topic

— Contents —

Page	Topic

— Contents —

Page	Topic

www.ingramcontent.com/pod-product-compliance
Lightning Source LLC
Chambersburg PA
CBHW061740050726
47598CB00002B/552